Petersen-Fleming

Puppy Training and Critters Too

32608

C
636.7
PX

## DATE DUE

| MAY 17, 2010 | |
| --- | --- |
| | |
| | |
| | |
| DISCARDED | |
| | |
| | |
| | |
| | |
| | |
| | |
| | |
| | |
| | |
| | |
| | PRINTED IN U.S.A. |

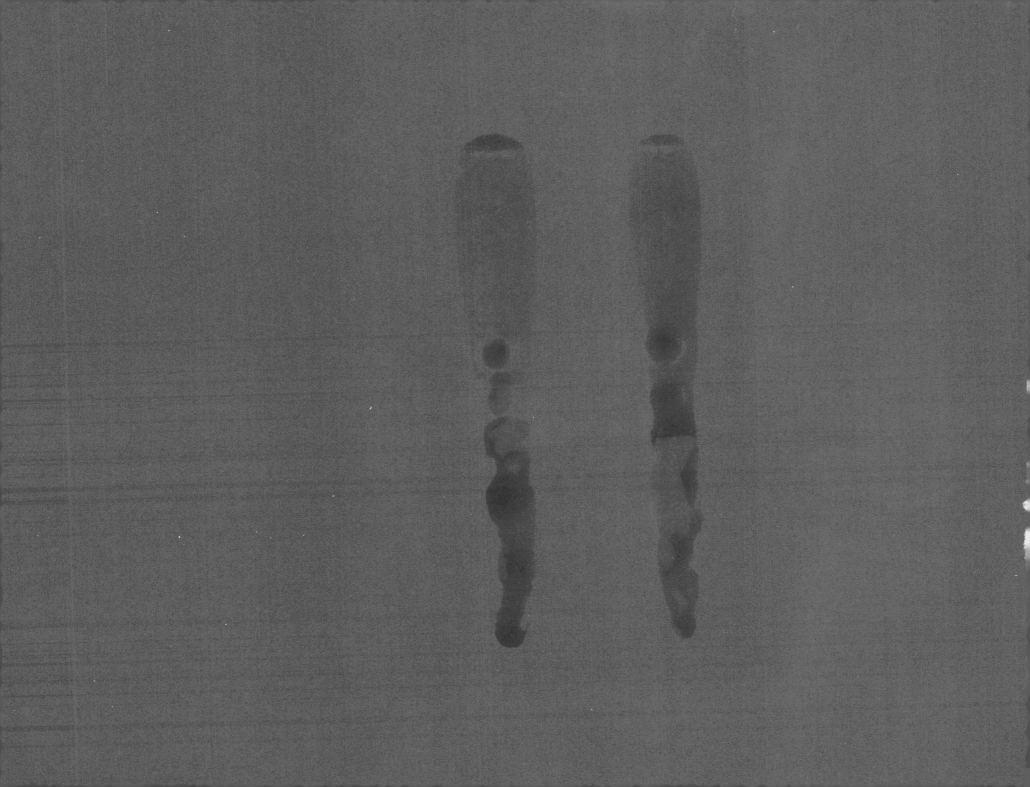

# PUPPY TRAINING

# AND CRITTERS, TOO!

# PUPPY TRAINING

## AND CRITTERS, TOO!

JUDY PETERSON-FLEMING

AND BILL FLEMING

PHOTOGRAPHS BY DARRYL BUSH

TAMBOURINE BOOKS, NEW YORK

FOR OUR RAY OF SUNSHINE, CIERA

# acknowledgments

The authors would like to thank the animals and trainers of Marine World Africa USA, a unique wildlife park and oceanarium in Vallejo, California, for their help.

Since 1968, Marine World has introduced the wonders of the animal world to over twenty-eight million visitors, including twelve million children spanning two generations. The park features animals of land, sea, and air in show performances, innovative exhibits, participatory attractions, and remarkable one-on-one encounters between animals, trainers, and guests.

Marine World Africa USA serves as a showcase for the many wonderful relationships that can exist between humans and animals. The park is owned by the Marine World Foundation, a nonprofit organization devoted to furthering people's understanding and appreciation of our world's wildlife.

We would also like to thank all of the children photographed in this book. Their patience and closeness to their pets made this book possible.

Finally, thanks to Brian and Cameron Reingold-Reiss, for letting Deb use her creativity!

# note to parents

Training a puppy is an experience that can bring the whole family closer together. Just as the trainers in this book work as a team while training exotic animals, your family will need to work together to train your new pet. Everyone in the family can become involved. Even the youngest children can participate by repeating the commands, such as saying "Come" when calling the puppy.

Your children will learn many interesting facts about wild animals while learning how to train their puppy. It will be exciting to them to use the same methods that trainers use with exotic animals.

It is important to remember that a trained pet is well behaved and can participate in family outings. Training your puppy is a great family activity that will give you greater enjoyment of your pet.

**N**OW THAT YOU KNOW HOW TO CARE FOR YOUR PUPPY, IT'S TIME TO LEARN HOW TO TRAIN YOUR PET. SEEING HOW TRAINERS WORK WITH WILD ANIMALS WILL HELP. ONCE YOU HAVE TRAINED YOUR PUPPY, YOU WILL BE ABLE TO ENJOY EACH OTHER'S COMPANY IN MANY PLACES.

**DOGS CAN'T SWEAT TO
COOL OFF THE WAY PEOPLE
DO, EXCEPT THROUGH
THEIR PAWS.**

If you follow the simple instructions in this book, you can learn how to train your puppy. Before starting, your puppy needs to become familiar with you. A good way is to let him sniff your hand and get to know your scent. During training, you and your puppy will become best friends and will be able to do many things together.

IN THE WILD, SQUIRREL MONKEYS LIVE IN TREES AND RARELY COME DOWN TO THE GROUND.

Suzy, a young squirrel monkey, has been working with this trainer for several years. Now Suzy completely trusts her trainer. They are able to go all over the park and play in many exciting areas together. The trainer uses the same methods to train Suzy that you will use with your puppy.

9

BY THE TIME PUPPIES ARE
FOUR WEEKS OLD, THEY
WEIGH ABOUT SEVEN TIMES
MORE THAN AT BIRTH.

It is *very* important for you to go
very s-l-o-w-l-y when training
your puppy. If you try to rush
your puppy, she will only get
confused, and it will take her
longer to learn new tasks.

AFRICAN ELEPHANTS USE THEIR LARGE EARS TO FAN THEMSELVES TO COOL OFF, AND TO BRUSH INSECTS AWAY FROM THEIR EYES.

Every time Judy's trainer teaches her something new, he goes through each step very slowly. Like your puppy, this young elephant must try several times before she will understand what the trainer wants her to do. Because Judy's trainer never hurries her, learning new things is fun, and Judy is able to learn much faster.

CERTAIN DOGS ARE NOT ABLE
TO BARK. THEY BELONG TO A
BREED CALLED BASENJI.

Animals learn by doing the same things over and over. When you train your puppy, you will need to repeat an exercise many times. First, pick *one* word as the command for each new behavior. *Repeat* this word many times during the training. For example, this boy says "Speak" several times to his puppy while teaching him to bark. He *never* changes the word to "Talk" or "Bark," but always uses the same command. Remember, if you're relaxed and enjoying the training, so will your puppy!

This young sea lion, Gunther, has learned many different behaviors from his trainer. Now he can enjoy a variety of activities and always knows what his trainers want him to do. When Gunther was learning, his trainers repeated the same behavior many times, always using the *same* commands.

SEA LIONS CAN MAKE A WIDE VARIETY OF SOUNDS, INCLUDING BARKING, SNORTING, ROARING, AND SNEEZING.

A DOG HAS SUCH KEEN HEARING THAT IT CAN DISTINGUISH THE SOUND OF THE FAMILY CAR FROM ALL OTHERS ON THE STREET.

*Never yell* commands at your puppy when training her. This will only scare her and make it very difficult for her to learn. Always use a gentle but *firm* voice when giving your puppy a command. The voice you use during training should be stronger and firmer than the voice you use when playing or when praising your puppy.

SLOTHS ARE THE SLOWEST MAMMALS ON EARTH. THEY LIVE IN TREES AND MOVE *VERY SLOWLY* FROM BRANCH TO BRANCH IN SEARCH OF FOOD.

The trainer is telling this baby sloth, Siesta, to "Stay" so he doesn't let go of her. She always uses a gentle but strong voice, so Siesta knows she's serious, but doesn't become afraid.

15

DOGS CAN SMELL CERTAIN SCENTS OVER *ONE MILLION* TIMES BETTER THAN PEOPLE CAN.

*Always* reward your puppy after he has done what you've asked him to do. Tell him how well he's done by giving him one of his favorite treats, along with several loving hugs and pats. Rewarding your puppy will make training enjoyable for him, so he will want to do it again.

# and critters, too!

This trainer is rewarding Stormy, a bottle-nosed dolphin, with her favorite fish treat, a herring. Stormy loves learning new behaviors from her trainer because she always gets a toy or treat, or her favorite reward—a rubdown!

DOLPHINS FEED ON ALL TYPES OF FISH AND CAN EAT OVER TWENTY-FIVE POUNDS OF FISH IN A DAY!

YOUR PUPPY'S EYES ARE MUCH MORE SENSITIVE TO MOVEMENT THAN YOURS. A SHEEPDOG CAN SEE ITS MASTER GIVING HAND SIGNALS A MILE AWAY!

To make training the most fun for you and your puppy, the training time should be short. Watch your puppy for signs that she is losing interest, such as looking away or acting restless. Stop the training session as soon as you see these signs of boredom. If your puppy loses interest in the lesson, she will not enjoy herself, and will not be as excited to start again next time.

*Before* Kona, a llama, gets bored, the trainer will end the training session, just as you should do with your puppy. The trainer watches Kona closely while they work together. If Kona tries to wander off or stops watching the trainer, the trainer will end the session. As long as Kona is enjoying herself, the trainer keeps going.

IN THE WILD, LLAMAS LIVE IN SMALL GROUPS CONSISTING OF ONE MALE AND FIVE TO TEN FEMALES.

AROUND THE AGE OF FOUR MONTHS, A PUPPY STARTS TO GET ITS ADULT TEETH AND FEELS A NEED TO CHEW. GIVE YOUR PUPPY PLENTY OF CHEW TOYS DURING THIS TIME.

This boy is teaching his puppy not to chew on his father's slipper. Start teaching your puppy "No" when he's still very young. Whenever your puppy is doing something you don't want him to, tell him "No" in a firm voice. Always use the same firm tone of voice and the same word. It will confuse your puppy if you say other words, such as "Stop" or "Don't."

This trainer is telling Ollie, an orangutan, "No" for trying to sneak some bananas while the trainer wasn't looking. Ollie understands that he has done something wrong, because he was taught "No" when he was very young. Ollie does not get confused—his trainer always uses the same word and repeats it many times whenever Ollie does something wrong.

ORANGUTANS FEED MOSTLY ON FRUIT, BUT WILL ALSO EAT LEAVES, BARK, AND FLOWERS.

**ADULT DOGS HAVE
FORTY-TWO TEETH.**

From the day you first get your puppy, you must teach her not to bite. Even a little nip during playtime when she's very young should not be allowed. Every time your puppy opens her mouth close to any part of your body, say a firm "No." Soon she will learn that biting at any time is off-limits.

Young cheetahs have very sharp claws and teeth. This trainer is working with Keesha, teaching him not to bite. Because Keesha's trainer tells him "No" each time he tries to take a friendly nip, he will soon understand that he is

A CHEETAH'S BODY, JUST LIKE
A GREYHOUND'S, IS BUILT FOR
SPEED. WITHIN TWO SECONDS

MOST AVERAGE-SIZED DOGS
CAN JUMP FIVE OR SIX FEET
STRAIGHT UP.

Your puppy should not get in the habit of jumping up on you or anyone else. This bad habit can lead to scratched legs and dirty clothes as your puppy gets bigger. Repeating a stern "No" *every time* your puppy jumps up on you or family members will keep him from learning this bad habit.

A TIGER'S TONGUE IS SO ROUGH, IT CAN ACTUALLY LICK THE PAINT OFF A HOUSE.

Young Sampson's trainers have been teaching him not to jump up on them from a very early age. They want to avoid being scratched. A scratch from a tiger is much more serious than one from a puppy or kitten because a tiger's claws are strong enough to shred the bark off a tree! The trainer says a firm "No" and gently places the tiger back down in order to give Sampson the message to stop jumping up.

**MOST DOGS CAN RUN AT AN AVERAGE SPEED OF THIRTY MILES PER HOUR.**

When teaching your puppy to come to you, pick one word and always use that *same* word. Choose a word like "Come" or "Here." Do not use your puppy's name, because she will hear her name many other times from you and your family. You don't want to confuse your puppy about what you want her to do.

Start in a small area. Have some treats ready. Say your puppy's name to get her attention, then call her by saying "Come" or "Here." When she comes to you, give her a treat and a lot of praise. Repeat this many times and increase the distance from which you call your puppy. She will soon know to come to you whenever you tell her to.

Young Maggie knows to go to her trainers whenever she hears the word "Come." Her trainers always give her lots of praise and love when she comes to them. Maggie enjoys working with her trainers because she is always rewarded and given a lot of affection when she does what they ask her to do.

CHIMPANZEES ARE "KNUCKLE-WALKERS"—THEY WALK ON THE BACKS OF THEIR HANDS AND KNUCKLES TO GIVE THEM SUPPORT.

PUPPIES CANNOT WAG THEIR TAILS RIGHT AFTER BIRTH. IT TAKES THEM BETWEEN ONE AND TWO MONTHS TO WAG THEIR TAILS.

There are many times when you will want your puppy to sit for a little while. You might tell him to "Sit" so he won't jump up or so you can put a collar and leash on him. It's also the first step before teaching him other commands, such as "Stay."

First get your puppy's attention while he's standing. Do this by making eye contact with him. Gently hold your puppy with one hand and softly push his bottom to the ground as you say "Sit." After your puppy holds this position for a few seconds, tell him he's a good boy and reward him with a treat. Repeat this several times, increasing the time you have him sit, so that eventually he can sit calmly for a couple of minutes.

ONLY MALE LIONS HAVE LONG MANES AROUND THEIR HEADS. THE THICK MANE PROTECTS THEIR NECK AND THROAT WHEN THEY FIGHT WITH OTHER MALES.

This handsome lioness, Nikka, learned to sit in one position so that she could get her favorite treat, a carton of milk! The lion and trainer have developed a mutual trust for one another because the trainer always gives all the lions love and praise while working with them.

ALL PUPPIES ARE BORN
BLIND AND DEAF. BETWEEN
THIRTEEN AND FIFTEEN DAYS,
THEY WILL BE ABLE TO SEE
AND HEAR.

It is important to teach your puppy to "Stay," so she doesn't run off when she's not supposed to. (Do not teach "Stay" until your puppy is very comfortable with "Sit.")

First, have your puppy sit, then walk a few steps away as you repeat "Stay." If your puppy starts to run toward you, say "No," then return your puppy to the same spot and have her sit again. Again, walk a few steps away as you repeat "Stay." When your puppy stays, *walk back* to her and give her treats and lots of praise. Repeat this many times while you increase the distance between you and your puppy. Be sure to stop the training if your puppy shows any signs of frustration, and try again later.

This trainer taught Frank the sea lion to stay in one spot. Frank stays so that the trainer has a chance to set up the toys. Once the toys are set up, Frank gets a reward and then dives in the pool to play!

SEA LIONS USE THEIR LONG WHISKERS AS FEELERS TO SENSE THEIR SURROUNDINGS IN MURKY WATERS.

DOGS SHARE THEIR INSTINCT TO BURY BONES WITH THEIR COUSINS, THE WOLVES. WOLVES WILL BURY LEFTOVER FOOD TO SAVE IT FOR LATER.

Fetch is a good game to teach your puppy, and a great way to help him stay fit. Start by setting a ball on the ground right below his mouth. When your puppy picks up the ball, say "Give it," and gently take the ball back. After he starts giving the ball back to you each time, throw it a short distance away and tell your puppy to "Fetch." Every time you throw the ball, slightly increase the distance you throw it.

It is important to tell your puppy to "Give it" whenever you ask for the ball. You will then be able to use this command anytime your puppy has something in his mouth you want him to give up, such as a slipper, another dog's bone, or a newspaper. This is also an extremely important command for your dog to know for safety reasons, in case he ever gets something in his mouth that could harm him.

This macaw, Benny, was trained to retrieve things and give them back to his trainer. The exercise helps Benny to keep up his flying skills, and is a great way for him to stay in shape.

MACAWS HAVE STRONG BEAKS THEY USE FOR CRACKING NUTS OPEN. THEIR BEAKS ARE SO STRONG THAT THEY CAN ACTUALLY SNAP A BROOMSTICK IN HALF.

**YOUR PUPPY WILL START TO BARK AT ABOUT THREE WEEKS OLD.**

Before you start training your puppy to walk on a leash, she should already be comfortable wearing a collar. Once she's used to her collar, you can make wearing a leash comfortable and positive. Start by putting on the leash and holding the other end so that it's loose. *Never* hold the leash tight so that you're pulling on your puppy. Run around and play with your puppy until she feels comfortable wearing the leash.

This cheetah, Arthur, is trained to walk on a leash, so that he and his trainer can investigate many places in the park where he lives. Because new things make cheetahs nervous, the trainer introduces Arthur to the leash slowly. Before they start walking, the trainer shows the cheetah the leash and lets him sniff it and push at it with his paws. Once Arthur has done this, the trainer will put the leash on and praise and pet him. This makes wearing the leash a positive experience for the cheetah.

**THE DARK LINE UNDER A CHEETAH'S EYE HELPS TO ABSORB THE GLARE OF THE HOT SUN.**

**MOST DOGS REACH FULL
MATURITY BY THE TIME THEY
ARE SIX MONTHS OLD.**

Now that your puppy is content *wearing* a leash, it is time to teach him to *walk* on a leash. It is important to teach this to your puppy, so that he will be able to accompany you away from home. Start by holding the end of the leash with your right hand and the middle of the leash with your left hand. Your puppy should *always* be on your left side. Start walking slowly with your puppy next to you. If he stops, say "Heel," and tug gently on the leash. This will teach your puppy to walk beside you. Remember to keep these sessions short. Make walking on a leash fun for your puppy by taking him to new places each time.

MOUNTAIN LION AND TIGER CLAWS GO BACK INSIDE THEIR PAWS, JUST LIKE A HOUSE CAT'S DO. BUT A CHEETAH'S CLAWS ARE ALWAYS OUT, JUST LIKE YOUR PUPPY'S.

These trainers spent many hours working with Keesha and Mara on their leashes, and now the two of them can walk anywhere together. The trainers taught the big cats how to walk on a leash the same way you will teach your puppy, except instead of saying "Heel," they tell the cats to "Come up." Now they can go out and look for new trees to climb and visit a variety of other animals in the park.

UNLIKE TIGERS, WHO SPEND MOST OF THEIR LIVES ALONE, DOGS ARE SOCIAL ANIMALS. THEY NEED COMPANIONSHIP, AND YOUR COMPANY IS VERY IMPORTANT TO THEM.

While training your puppy, you will spend a lot of time together and be able to share many fun outings. This time together will build a friendship and bond between the two of you that you can't develop any other way. Through training your puppy, you will establish a very special life-long relationship.

Printed in Hong Kong by South China Printing Company (1988) Ltd.
The text type is 12 pt. Century Light.

Library of Congress Cataloging in Publication Data
Petersen-Fleming, Judy. Puppy training and critters, too! / by Judy Petersen-Fleming
and Bill Fleming ; photographs by Darryl Bush. — 1st ed.    p. cm.
Summary: Demonstrates how to train a puppy by comparisons
with how keepers train wild animals in captivity.
1. Puppies—Juvenile literature.  2. Animals—Juvenile literature. [1. Dogs—
Training.  2. Animals—Training.]  I. Fleming, Bill.  II. Bush, Darryl, ill.  III. Title.
SF426.5.P455 1996   636.7'0887—dc20   95-23031   CIP  AC
ISBN 0-688-13384-3 (trade).—ISBN 0-688-13385-1 (lib. bdg.)

1  3  5  7  9  10  8  6  4  2
First edition

Photograph on page 34 copyright © 1996 by Debra Reingold-Reiss.
All other photographs copyright © 1996
by Darryl W. Bush/Marine World Africa USA, Vallejo, California.